CY

by SCHULZ

Not Just Another Pretty Face

HarperHorizon
An Imprint of HarperCollins*Publishers*

HarperHorizon
An Imprint of HarperCollins*Publishers*

Produced by Jennifer Barry Design, Sausalito, CA
First published in 1998 by HarperCollins*Publishers* Inc.
http://www.harpercollins.com
Lucy: Not Just Another Pretty Face was published by HarperHorizon, an imprint of
HarperCollins*Publishers* Inc., 10 East 53rd Street, New York, NY 10022.

Creative and Editorial Director: Jennifer Barry
Editorial Assistant: Kristen Schilo
Design Assistant: Kristen Wurz
Production Manager: Dianne Walber

ISBN 0-06-107300-8

Printed in Hong Kong

1 3 5 7 9 10 8 6 4 2

Contents

Introduction

Lucy Van Pelt is the original dominant female character in *Peanuts*. She's Linus and Rerun's big sister. She's bossy and self-centered. She's in love with Schroeder, but her love is not returned. With Lucy, I really don't know if I like her or not, but I must admit that the strip certainly needs her. Sometimes, I think she is all bad, but maybe she is simply human.

Lately, Lucy has become a great source of satisfaction for me, but also a problem. When she was first introduced into the strip in 1952, she was simply a cute, doll-like figure with large round eyes. Jim Freeman, who was our editor at the time, suggested that I eliminate the large round eyes. Lucy began to develop her personality when I started to call her a fussbudget. In fact, at one time she possessed a trophy that named her the "World's Number One Fussbudget."

When characters work in a comic strip it is because one thing leads to another, and the very personality that you have given him or her starts to provide you with more ideas. The fussier Lucy became, the more ideas she gave me. Her persecution of poor Linus, after he came along, accounted for years and years of ideas.

Then came their little brother, Rerun. At first I was sorry I had brought him in. All I could think of doing with him was placing him on the back of his mother's bicycle. Lately, however, I have put him in kindergarten, which was probably inspired by our own grandchildren. Suddenly Lucy's personality has mellowed, and she has become the only *Peanuts* character to pay much attention to him. We have seen her playing games with Rerun and actually trying to

teach him a few things, but directly opposite of the outrageous teachings she used to push upon Linus.

This, then, is the problem—what do we do with Lucy? She seems no longer to be a fussbudget, but we also don't want her to be too nice. Anyway, comic strips go along from day to day and fortunately it is nothing too serious to worry about.

Charles M. Schulz
Charles M. Schulz, 1998

9

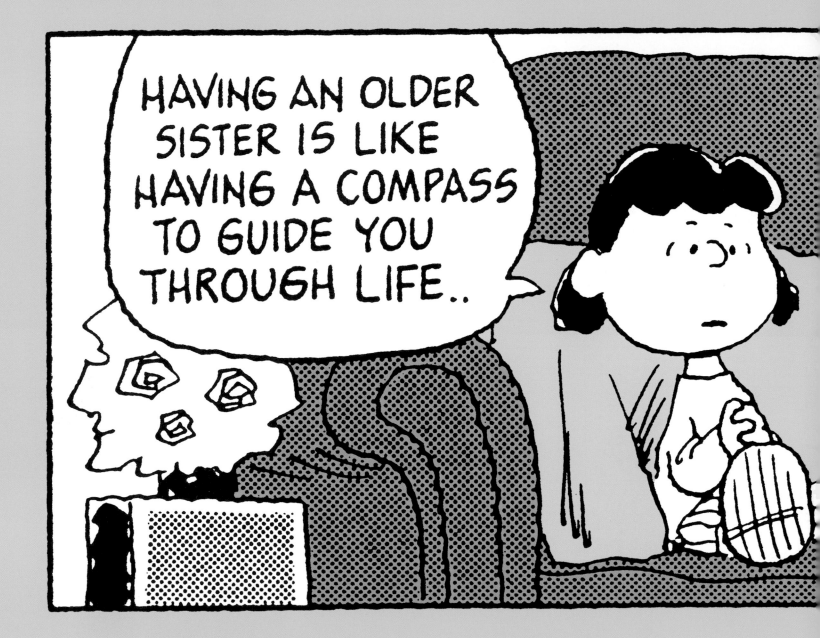

I Love Lucy

She's stubborn! She's a know-it-all! She's crabby! She's bossy (but don't say it to her face)! Lucy Van Pelt is the girl everybody loves to hate and hates to love. She's the domineering older sister and world-famous psychiatric advice dispenser who prides herself on her brains and good looks. She's "in your face" and her attitude is always maddening. Yet, when compared to her wishy-washy friend Charlie Brown, or her thumb-sucking, blanket-carting brother Linus, how can anyone not love Lucy?

The only thing Lucy is missing is the attention of her "boyfriend" pianist, Schroeder. Still, day after day, she leans on Schroeder's very baby grand, expecting him to declare his love for her. The most she gets is a kiss from that kiss-stealing beagle, Snoopy. Oh, and sometimes she gets the ol' ivories pulled out from under her, particularly when she mentions marriage. Nobody else would come back for more, but Lucy's unwavering optimism (and unflinching stubbornness) is what makes her so appealing.

13

She's The Boss

As Linus and Rerun's older sister, Lucy gets tons of practice telling her brothers what to do and how to do it. She's used to getting her way. Lucky for her, everybody's used to giving it to her. Whether she's ordering Linus to get her a drink or get out of "her" beanbag chair, or even telling her little league baseball team manager how to play, she's the boss. However, don't you dare call her bossy—she can stand anything but being called bossy!

When Lucy speaks, people must listen! The world would be a much better one if everyone would just listen to her—a simple philosophy spoken by an outspoken gal. Her word of mouth is not free of charge, however, so she is often found at her psychiatric booth dispensing her 5 cents' worth of flawless advice and requisite criticism. Lucy's new age pragmatism has been hailed most ardently by Lucy herself, of course, and also by her legion of fans—how else could she maintain a profitable business for forty years!

OPINIONS - 5¢
THOUGHTS FOR THE DAY - 10¢
SOUND ADVICE - 25¢

33

BOSSY BOSSY BOSSY
BOSSY BOSSY BOSSY
BOSSY BOSSY BOSSY BOSSY

BOSSY BOSSY BOSSY BOSSY
BOSSY BOSSY BOSSY BOS
BOSSY
BOSSY

Born Crabby

In addition to being first-born and chief controller, Lucy has also been crabby since birth! Lucy the crab is always "in" and ready to yell, but don't think it comes naturally to her. As Lucy says, "Crabby looks take a lot of practice." She spends time and energy practicing the fine art of crabbiness on her friends and family. Poor Linus knows that living with Lucy takes just as much hard work and patience as being the perfect crab—if not more.

When Lucy's not crabbing, she's probably sulking. She's a world-class sulker and sulks best in the family beanbag chair. Just like the rest of us, she can be thwarted by life's ups and downs; and since she's used to getting her way, you'd better stay out of it when Lucy's chips are down. Linus has even developed an early warning system to let everyone know to steer clear of Lucy when she's in one of her crabby moods. Will Lucy always be crabby? Maybe not, but she hopes so—and after all, practice makes perfect!

Born Crabby

53

CRABBY LOOKS

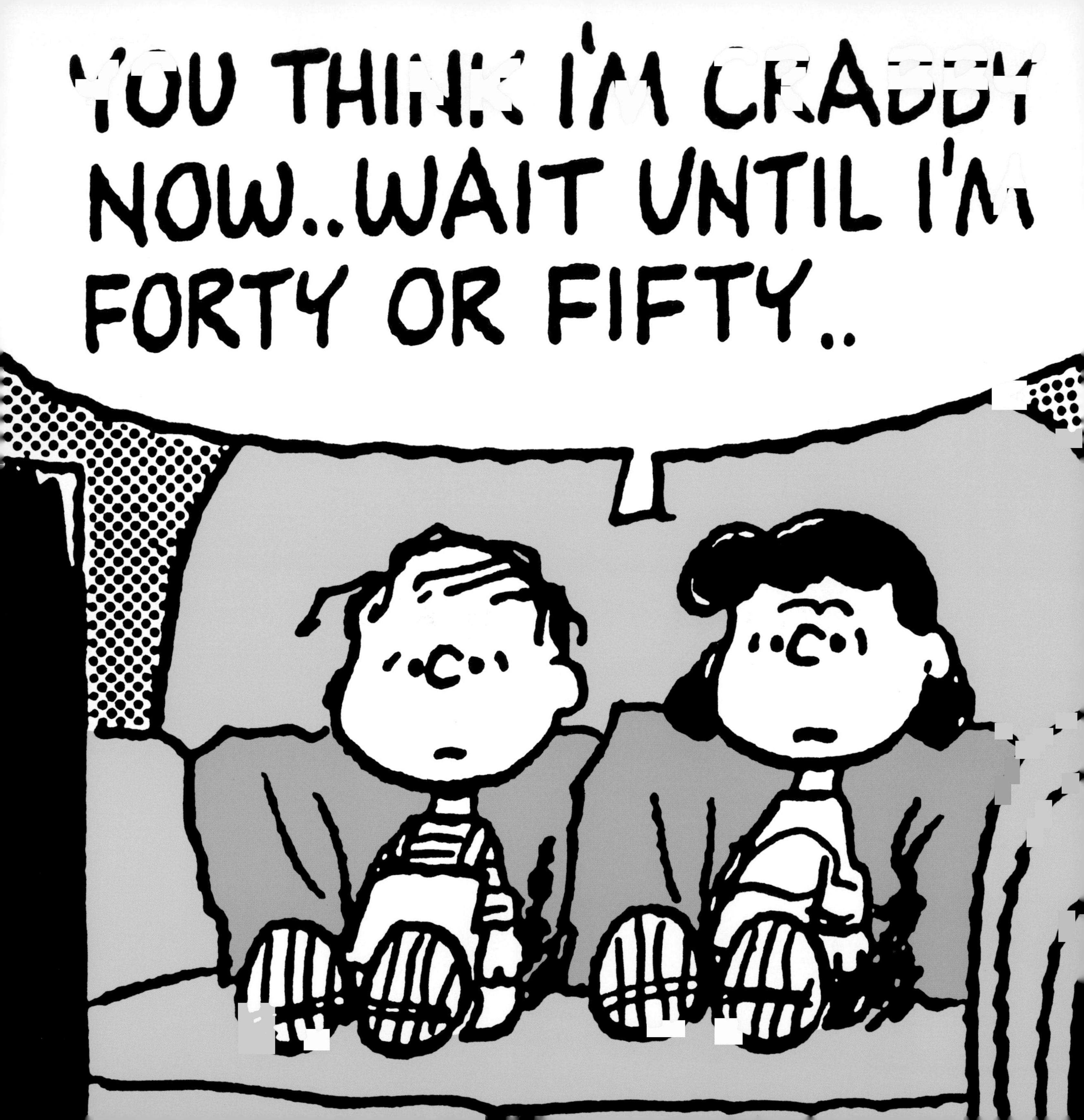
YOU THINK I'M CRABBY NOW..WAIT UNTIL I'M FORTY OR FIFTY..

Nobody's Perfect

Lucy is always at the center of things, even while playing right field! Perfect as she is most of the time, the one place she can be humbled—momentarily, anyway—is on the baseball field. She may not be a pro at America's favorite pastime, but she's an expert when it comes to creative excuses for missing fly balls and unsolicited advice for the pitcher. Her unrequited love for Schroeder keeps distracting her on the field of dreams, and since Lucy knows not the meaning of the word "no," she keeps her flirting game going with her pitches to catch the catcher.

Well, nobody's perfect, not even Lucy, but her willful character makes life interesting, very interesting indeed. Without her to keep them on their toes, things would be humdrum for Charlie Brown, Schroeder, Linus, Rerun, and Snoopy. Thankfully she *is* always around, demonstrating to the world that *she's not just another pretty face!*

71

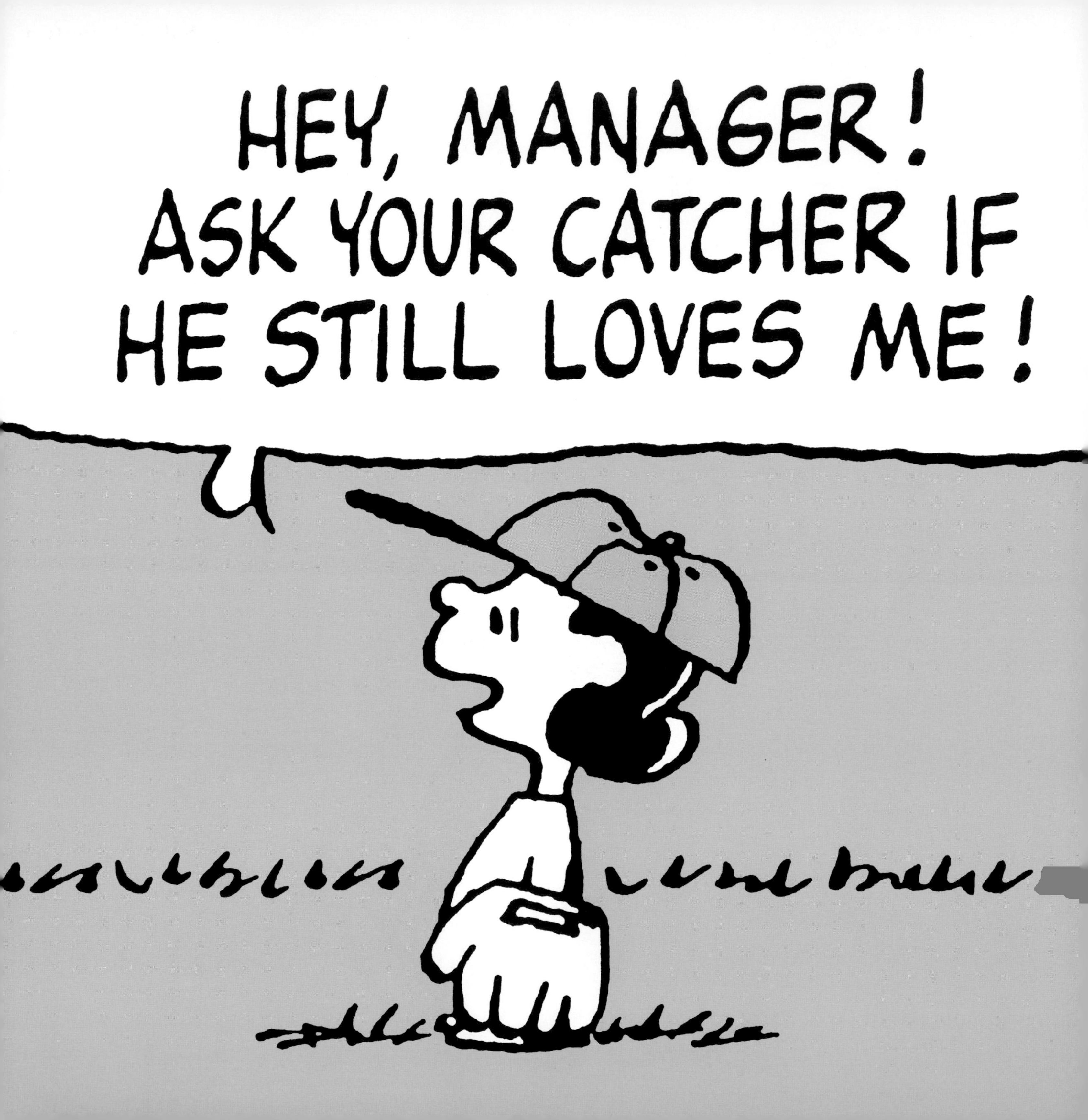
HEY, MANAGER! ASK YOUR CATCHER IF HE STILL LOVES ME!

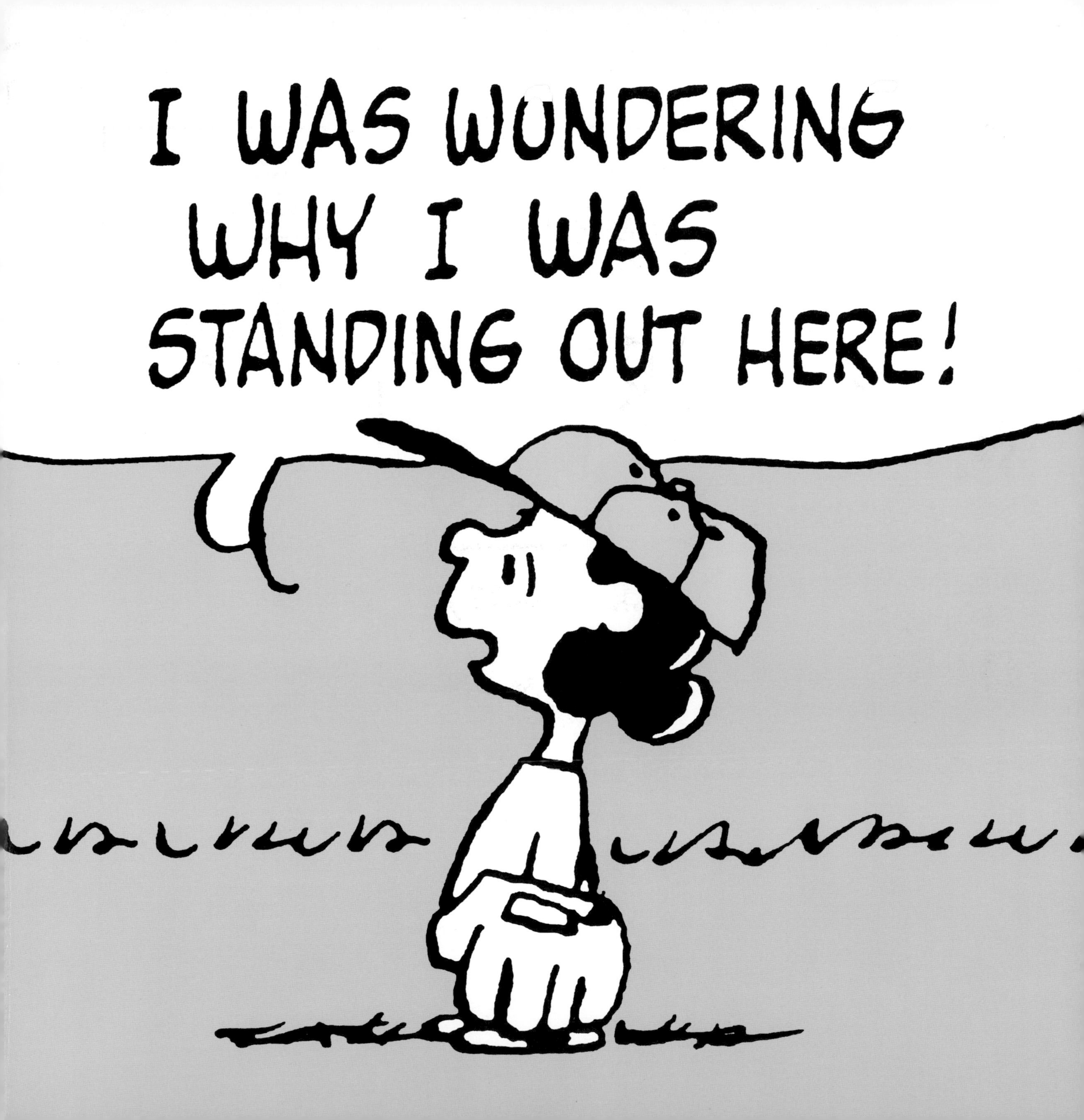
I WAS WONDERING WHY I WAS STANDING OUT HERE!

When You're Perfect, You Have To Do Everything Yourself Born Crabby This Is Not A Lemonade Stand! The Doctor Is In You're A Blockhead! This Case Could Make Me Famous Just Relax, And Don't Think So Much Life Is A Lot Like A Grocery Cart Crabby Looks Take A Lot Of Practice Maybe You're Normal, Maybe You're Not Psychiatrists Don't Give Rain Checks! Hope Got In My Eyes Lucy's Here Let's Just Say You and I Are Married . . . Pay Attention To Me! Sit Up Straight, You're Slouching

When You're Perfect, You Have To
This Is Not A Lemonade Stand! The
Case Could Make Me Famous Just Re
A Lot Like A Grocery Cart Crabby
You're Normal, Maybe You're Not F
Hope Got In My Eyes Lucy's Here Le
Pay Attention To Me! Sit Up Straight,
When You're Perfect, You Have To
This Is Not A Lemonade Stand! The
Case Could Make Me Famous Just Re
A Lot Like A Grocery Cart Crabby
You're Normal, Maybe You're Not F
Hope Got In My Eyes Lucy's Here Le
Pay Attention To Me! Sit Up Straight